THE PRAYING ATHLETE™

PHOTOGRAPHY

QUOTE BOOK - VOL 2

Robert B. Walker

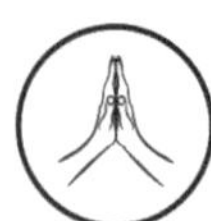

The Praying Athlete Photography Quote Book Volume 2

Published by The Core Media Group, Inc., P.O. Box 2037, Indian Trail, NC 28079.

Quotes written by Robert B. Walker. Photography by Robert B. Walker & Ashlyn Helms.
Cover and interior design by Ashlyn Helms.

Printed in the United States of America.

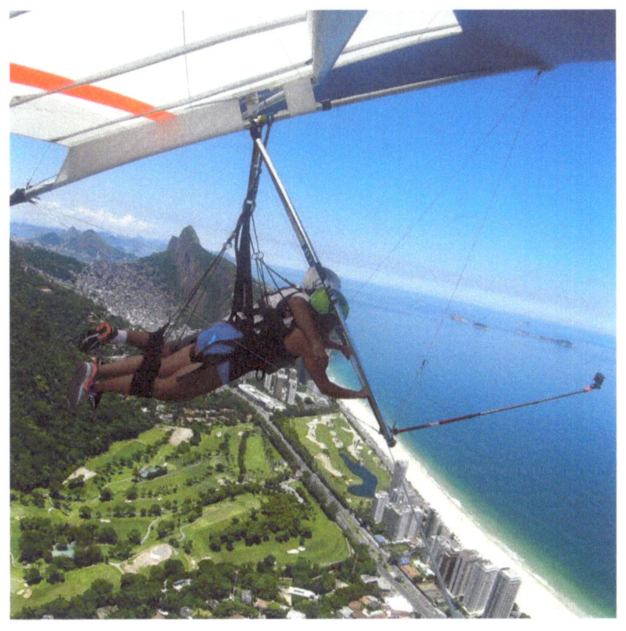

"SOAR! Enjoy the ride! Find that true friend who will encourage you, and take them with you! If you have that true friend, share these words and challenge them to go along with you, and you with them. If you cannot locate that true friend, go alone. God will allow your true friend to show up in His time! Be Blessed!"

"The path of yesterday has already been traveled. Find new ways and new roads to new opportunities."

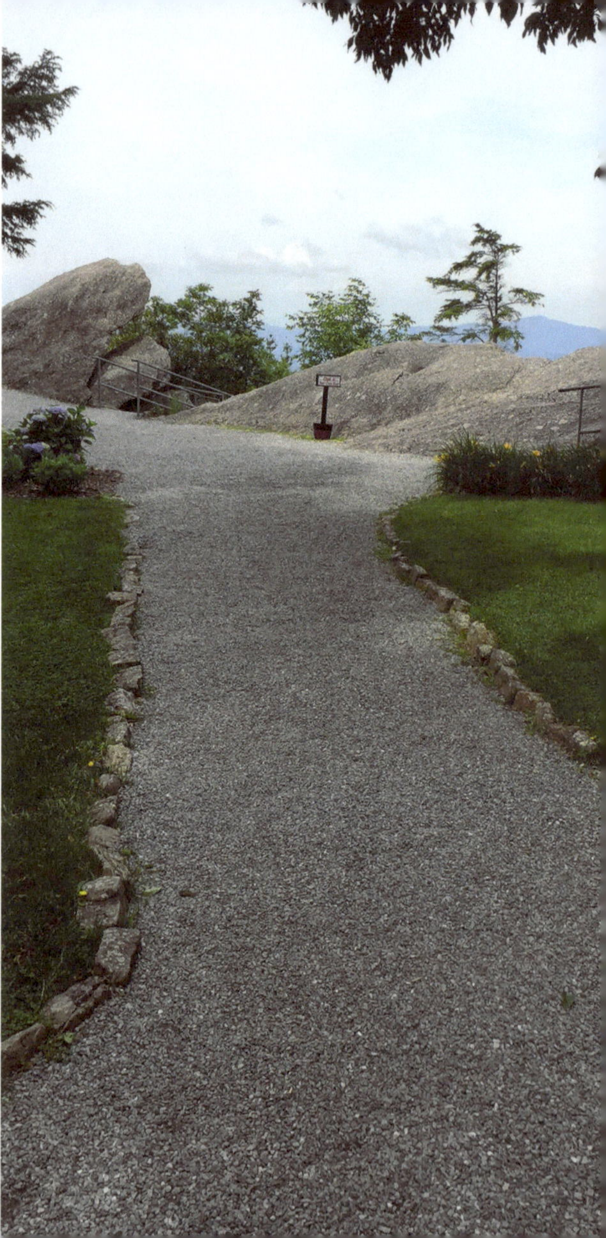

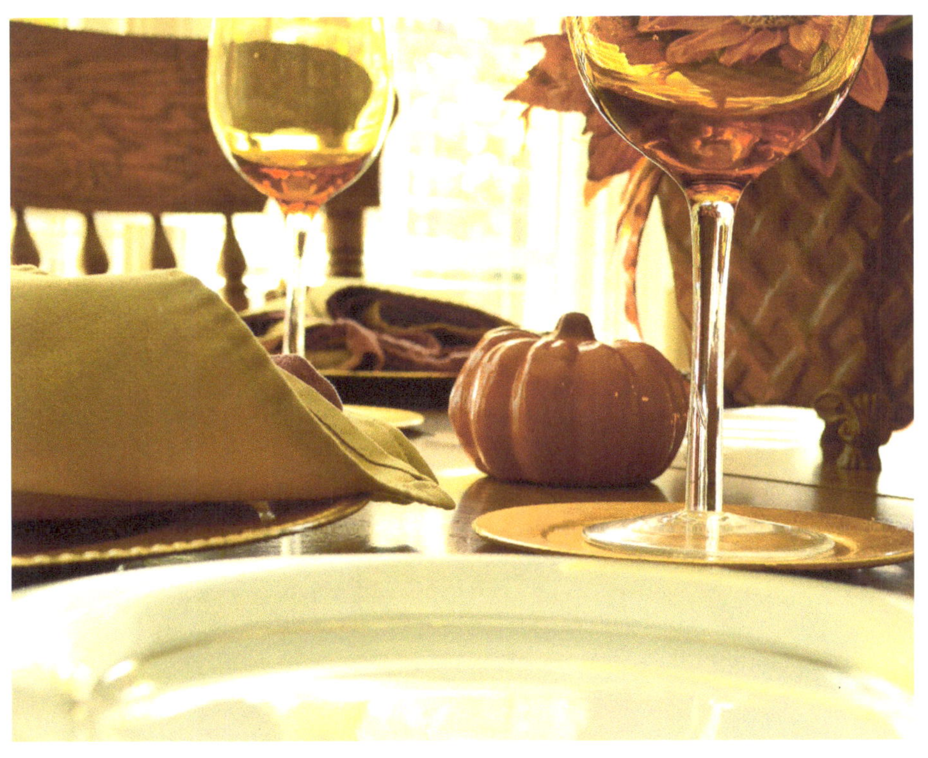

"Having the right recipe for life is critical. The best recipes are usually the ones you gain from friends, family, and generations. Ask what helped them in the game of life. You may find a few ingredients that can help you and your life."

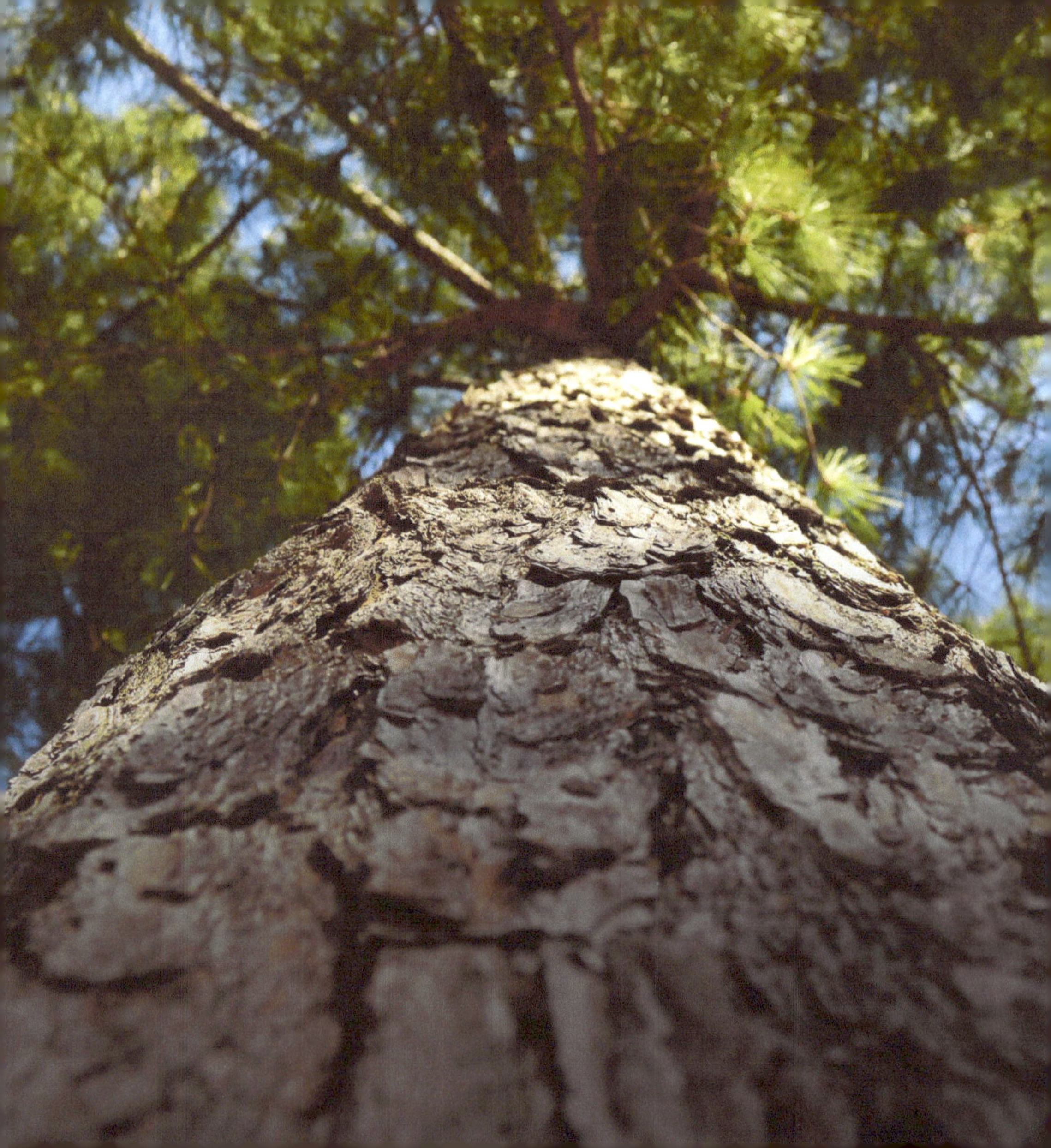

"You can soar to new heights and conquer any doubts or fears. You will fly to the destination called hope, where you will find comfort, peace, and confidence."

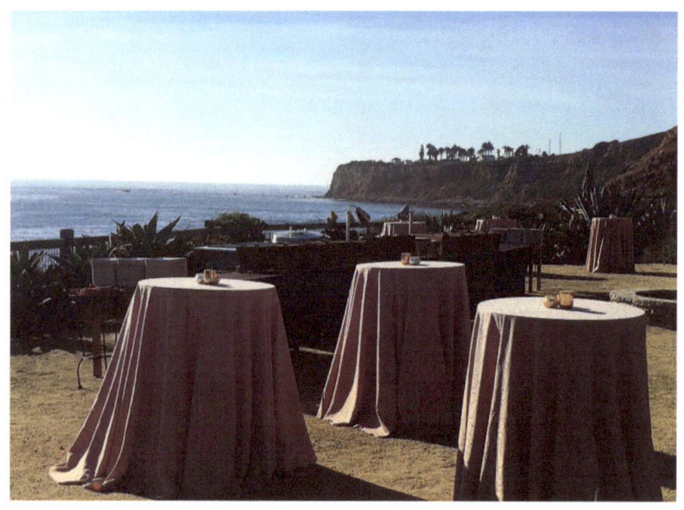

"Sometimes God is preparing a feast for you in a beautiful place. Stay true to who God created you to be and the desires He has put into your heart. Never settle for second best because He wants His best for you."

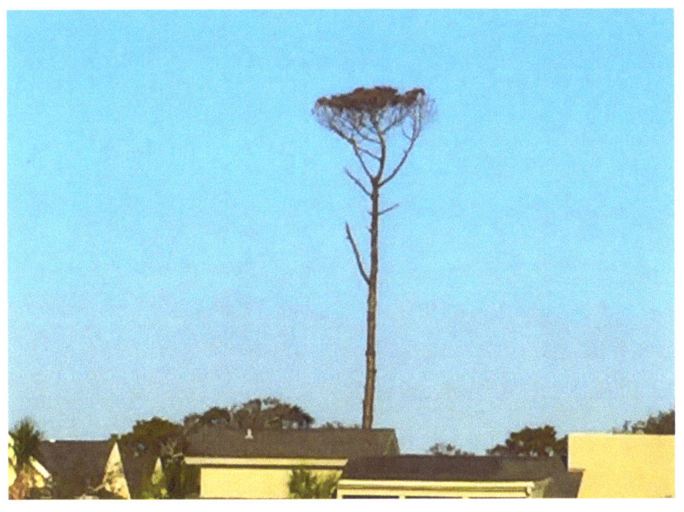

"Sometimes you have to take a stand and that may mean standing alone. You will stand out and people will take notice, but you will grow and become stronger. You will out pace the competition every time!"

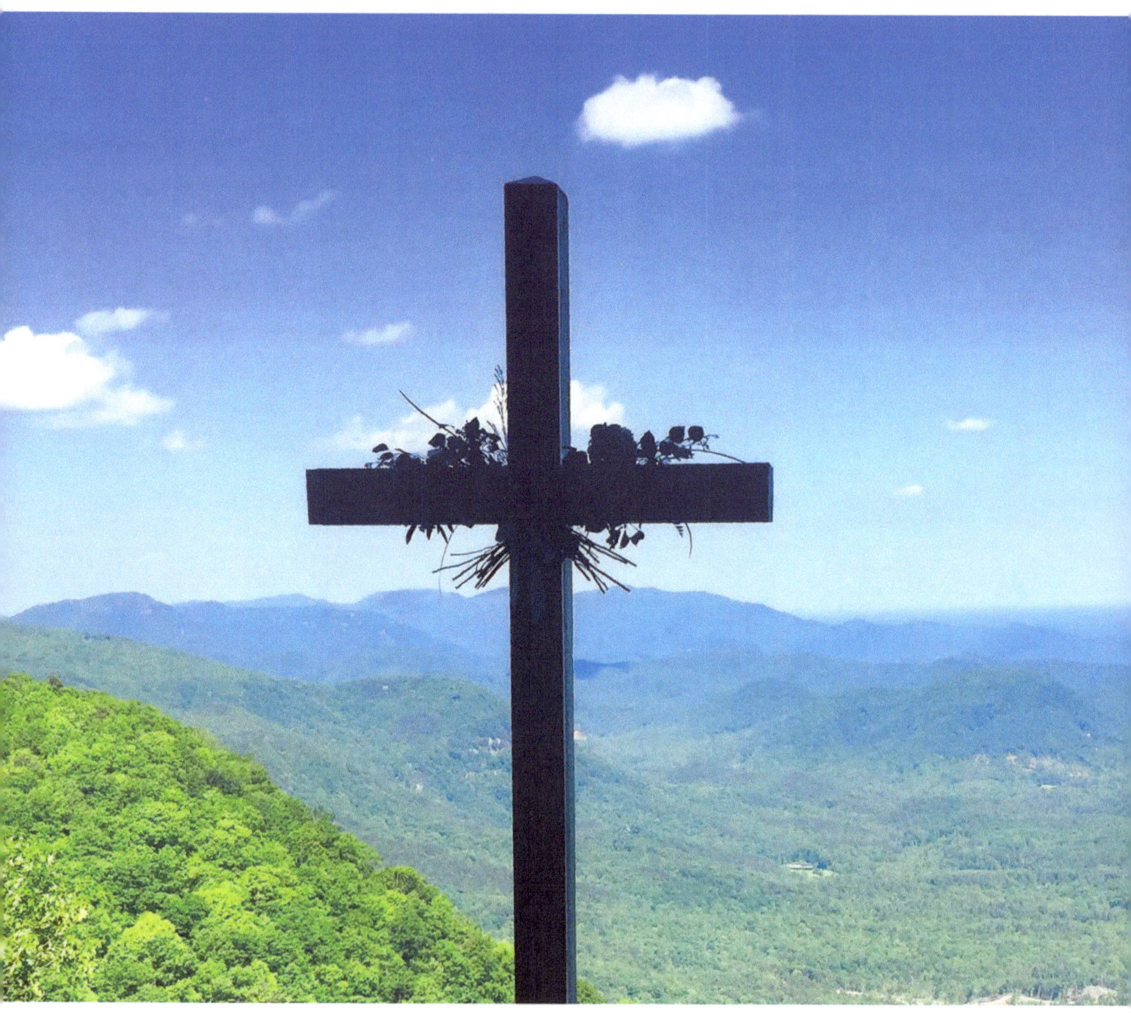

"Many times, we incarcerate ourselves with the feelings of yesterday and our past. That bondage will keep you not release you. However, you can unlock your new future and release yourself from yesterday by letting go of the people and feelings that do not propel you. You will then find new blessings and success for yourself."

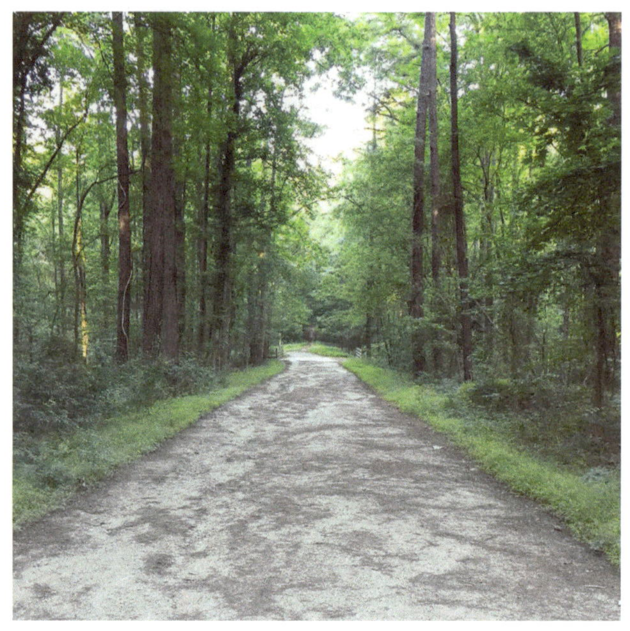

"Today is another step in the direction and path God has laid out for you. You are well prepared for this journey today. Embrace it with gladness and enthusiasm. The results are already in because you prepared for them even before today began. Enjoy and embrace the confidence that is within you today. All the best for the best day ever!"

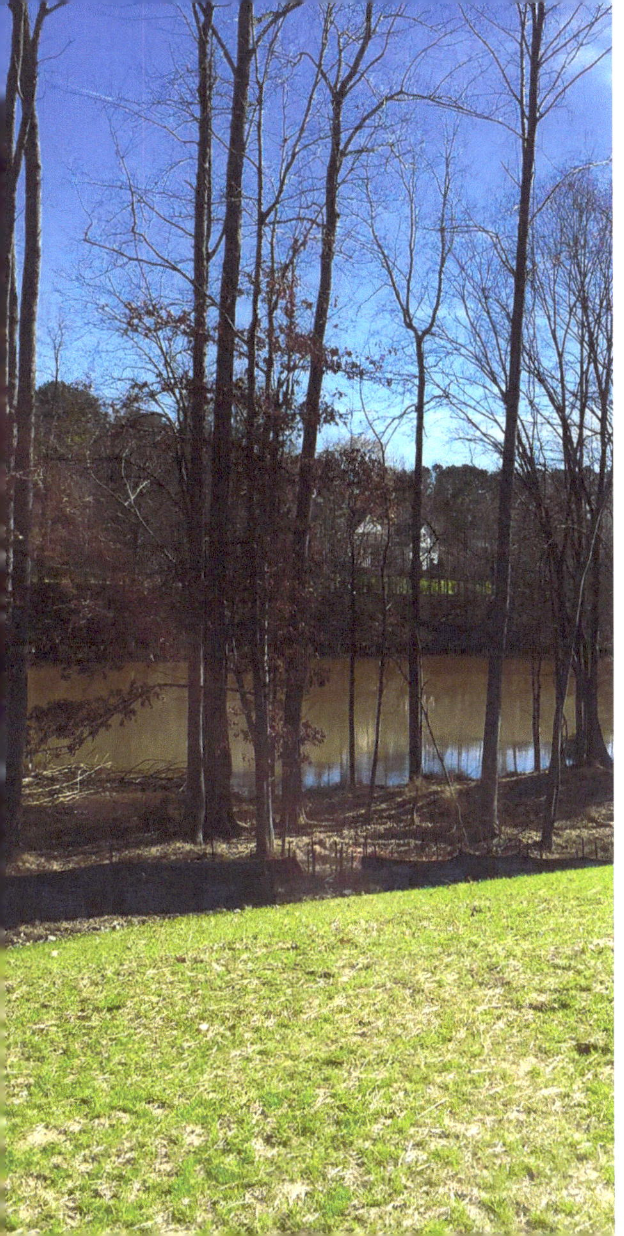

"Finding fish in a 5,000-acre lake can be very difficult. Finding your success will also be difficult, but it is out there; just don't stop looking for it."

"In time you will bloom
and reach the best
you. Keep doing
the things that keep
your roots healthy—
this is the only way
to reach your peak
performance."

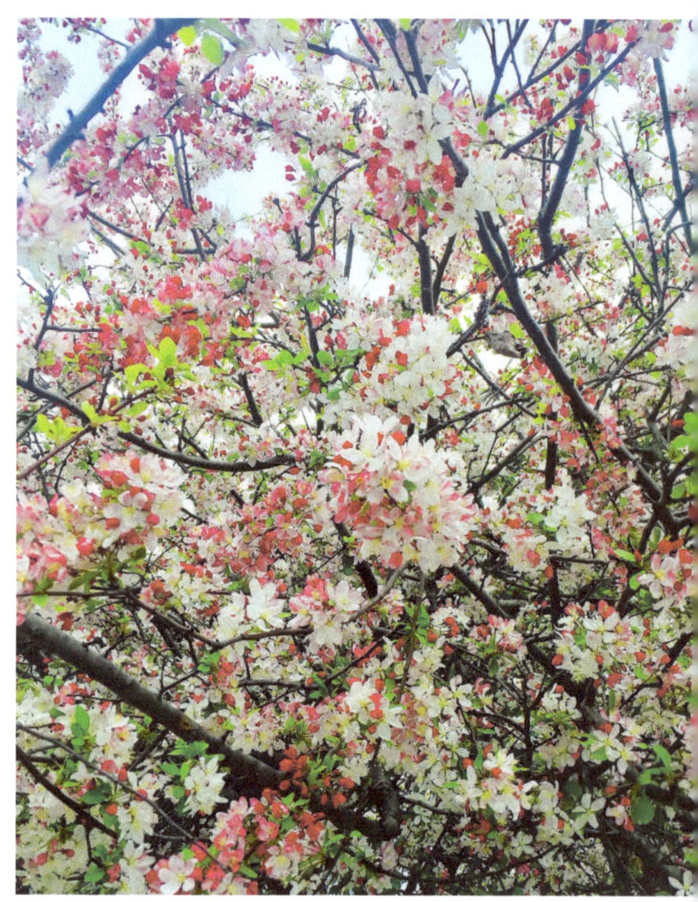

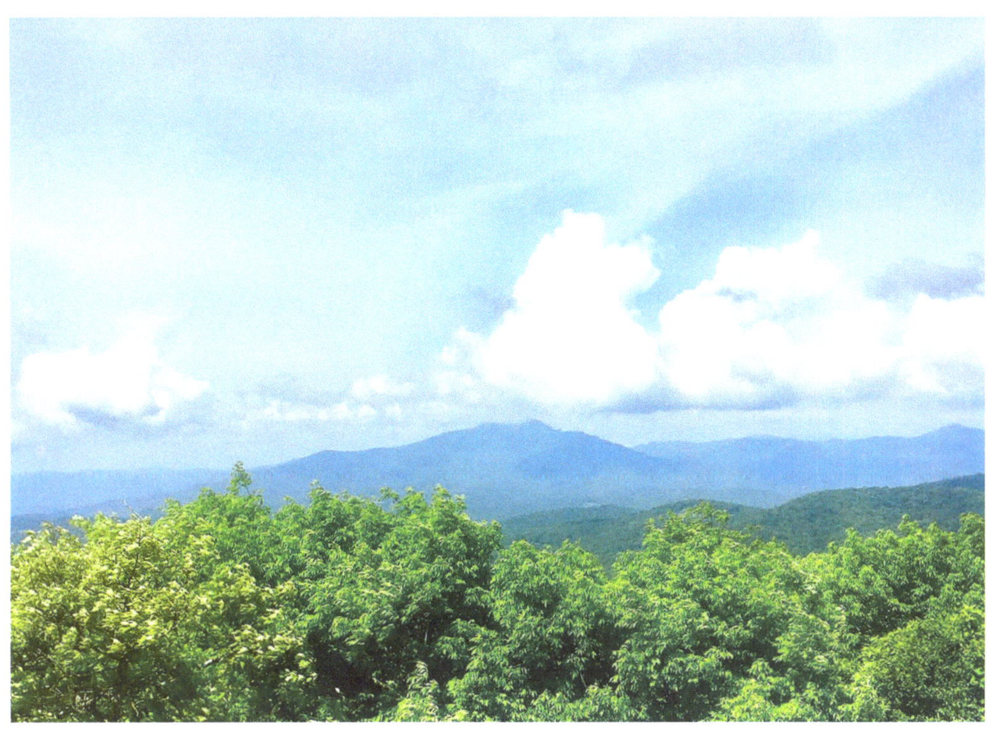

"Go for a walk, hear the birds. Go for a run, feel the heat. Go for a bike ride, feel the wind. Go for a drive, see the landscapes. Go on a flight, see the beauty from up high. Do all of these things to appreciate life and God's incredible creation."

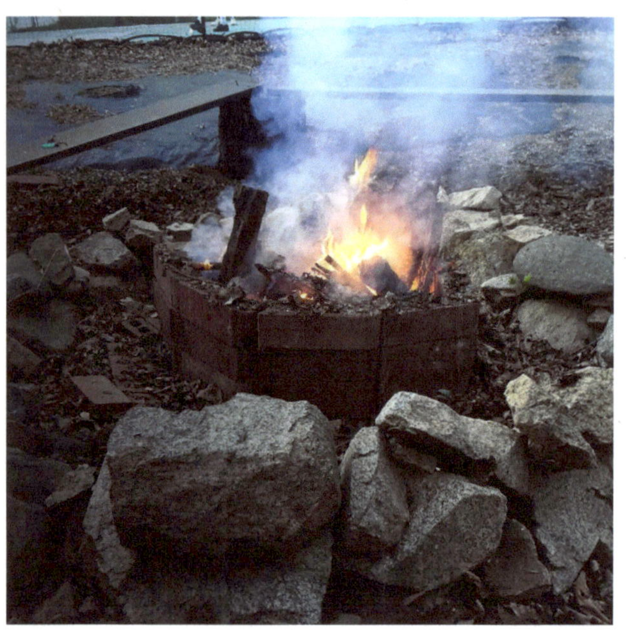

"Firefighters help to put out fires to save people and things. Are you willing to help people put out fires in their own lives? It will require some heated battles, but someone has to help before the fire destroys more people and friends."

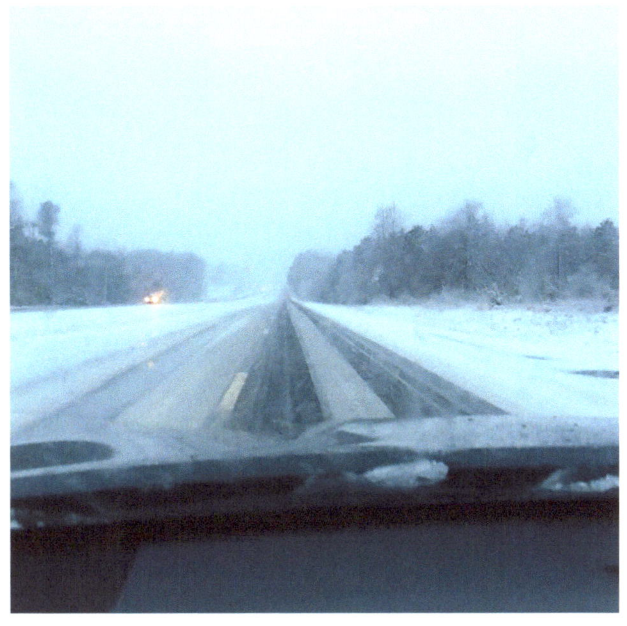

"The purpose of the speed limit is to control us. The speed at which you live life is your own choice."

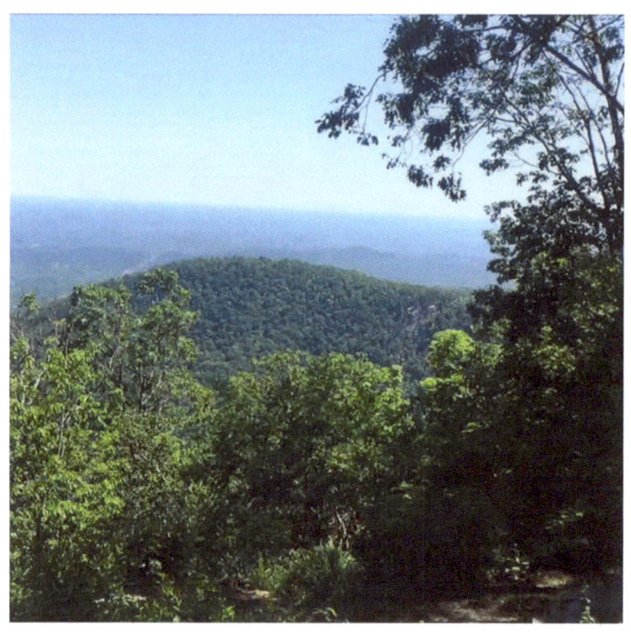

"Things change. In the winter, these trees will be brown and dead, but there is always life in the root. Plant your roots to withstand the tough times."

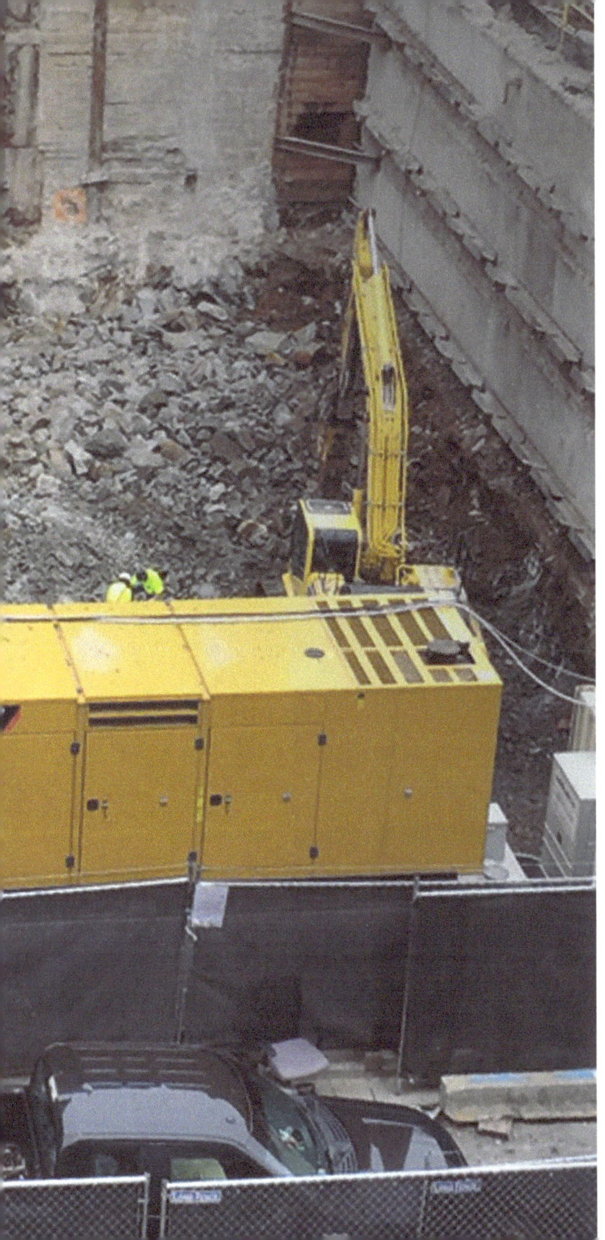

"Sometimes you need to dig deep to find what is troubling you, so you can heal and build a new and stronger foundation."

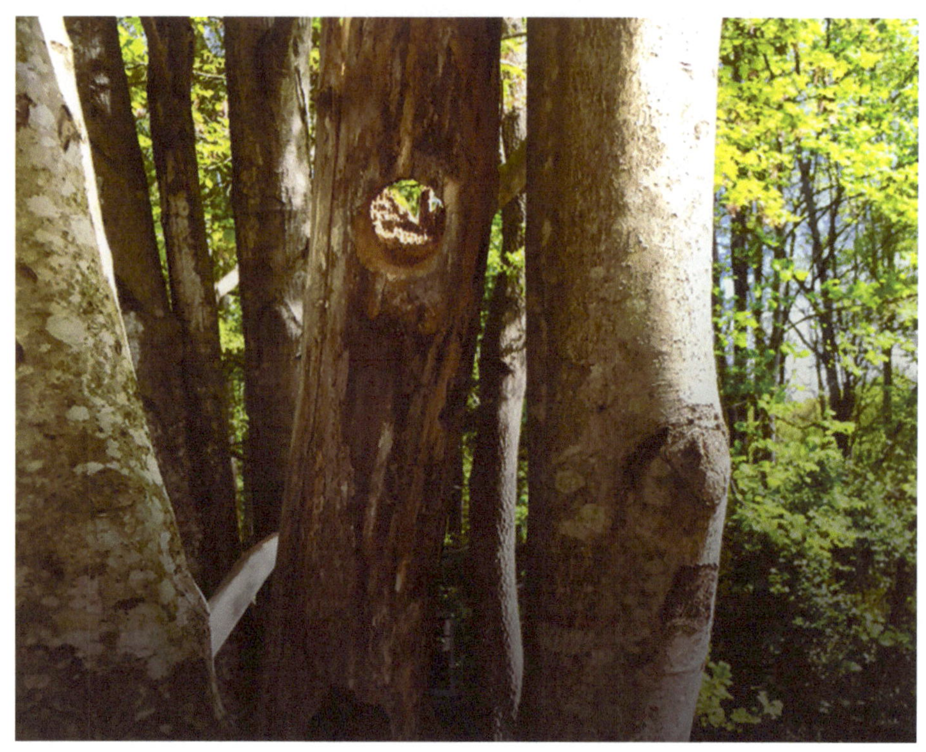

"Success does not happen in a day. You must keep pecking everyday to make it to the other side, one peck at a time. Woodpeckers peck away continuously until they receive the food they desire from the insects, but they also bore a hole for nesting. They give tremendous effort with great rewards—a home and food for their young and themselves. As you strive to achieve your daily goals, keep in mind that it will happen, but at the pace of one peck at a time. Keep Pecking!"

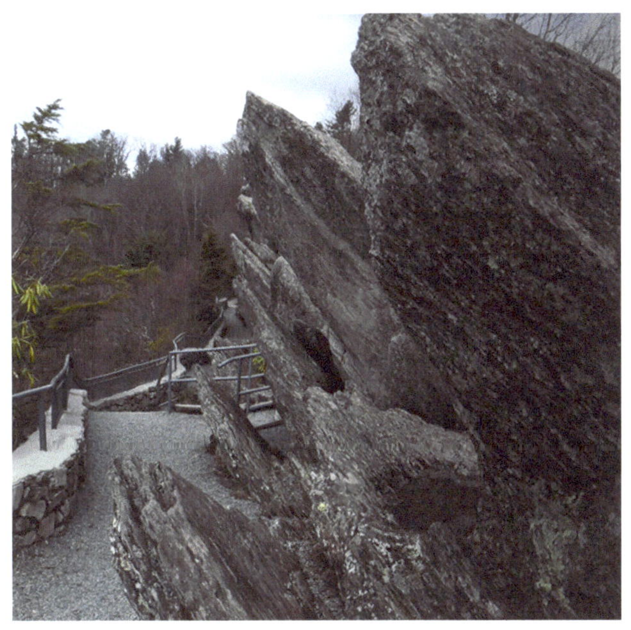

"Many things will crowd the path of life and the way may become rough, jagged and sharp. Those things make it more difficult to stay on course, however, never give in. Keep moving to the place you cherish and who you want to be. It may not be easy, but that is where your peace will lie."

"There are some things in life you cannot do alone—you need a team. Define what value is to you and build relationships based on those values. Prepare and select those that build and speak back into your life. You need each other more than you know."

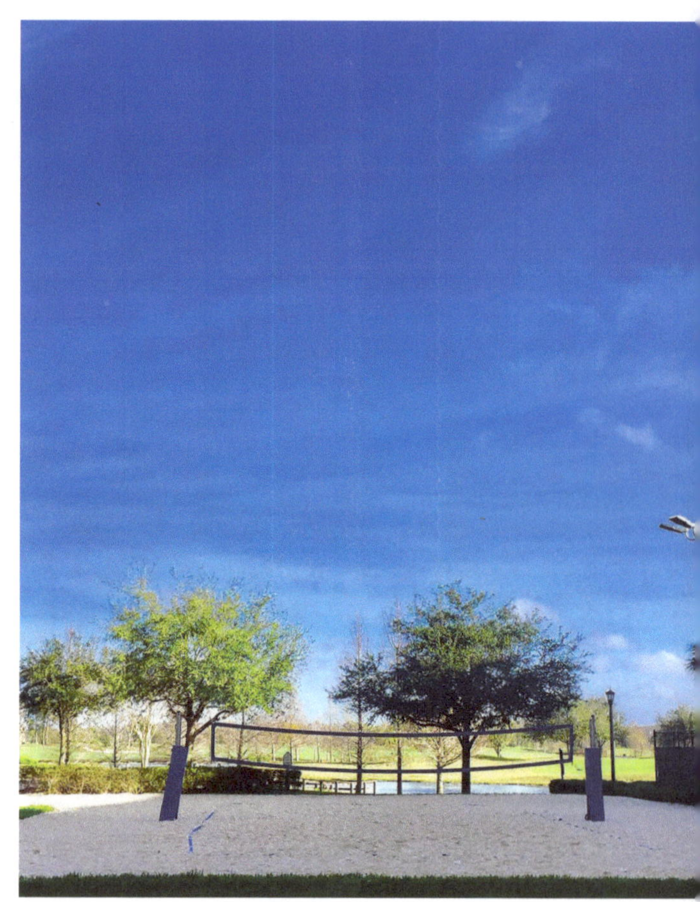

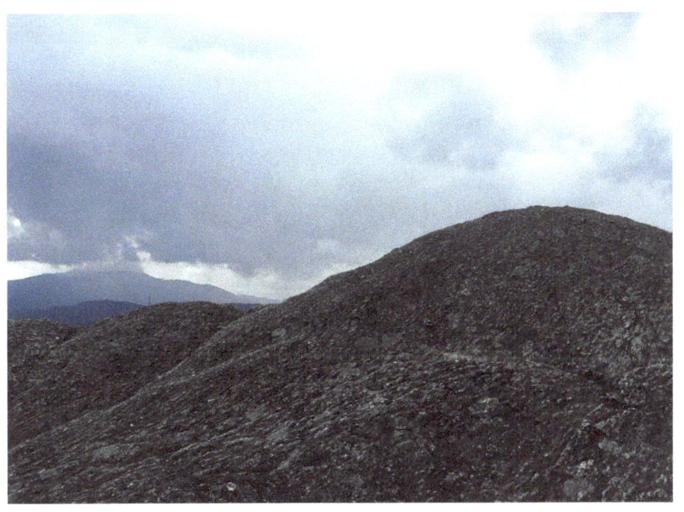

"You're almost there, keep climbing. Never give up on the climb. You will soon reach the other side. Once you are there it will be worth it! Promise!!"

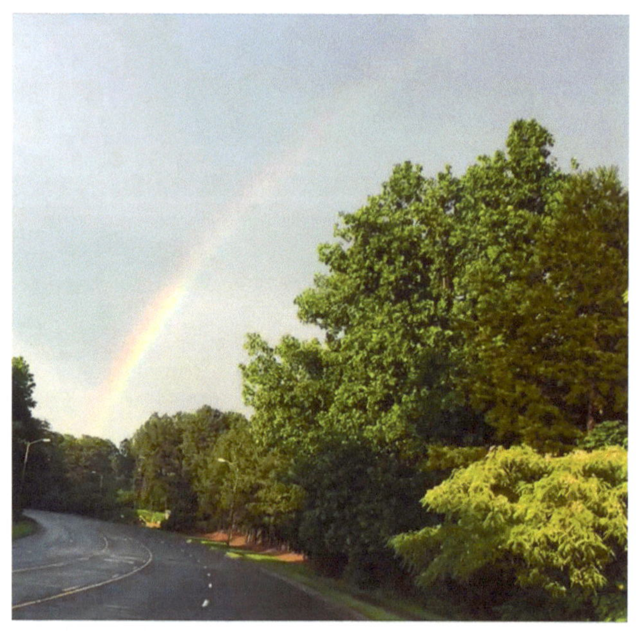

"Chase your dreams. Keep driving toward them. Why not? The action is in the chase."

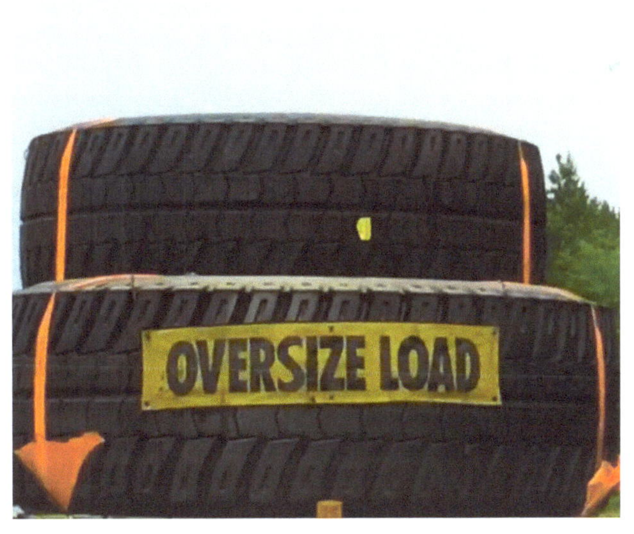

"As I travel, I see different things along the way. These have to be the biggest tires I have ever seen anywhere. I thought to myself, everything has a purpose and a plan. The truck was barely wide enough to carry the tires. These tires will only fit a certain type of equipment. Remember, there is a plan for you. You have purpose and incredible meaning. Embrace the pursuit of your purpose everyday."

"What do you have flowing into your life?
Will it lead you to where you want to go?
Find the right flow with the people and things
you allow into your life."

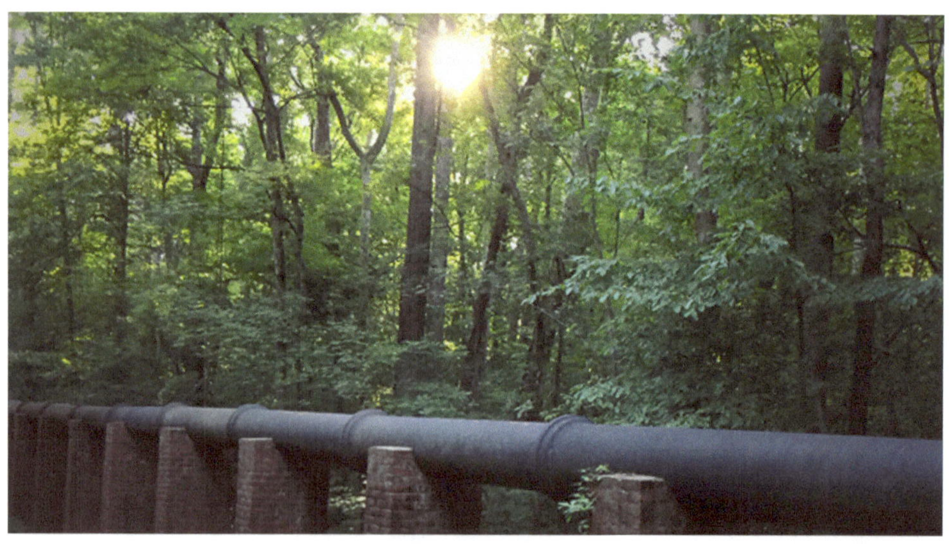

"You may be the only tree standing, but you have withstood the test of time and the storms of life. Keep standing even if you are alone."

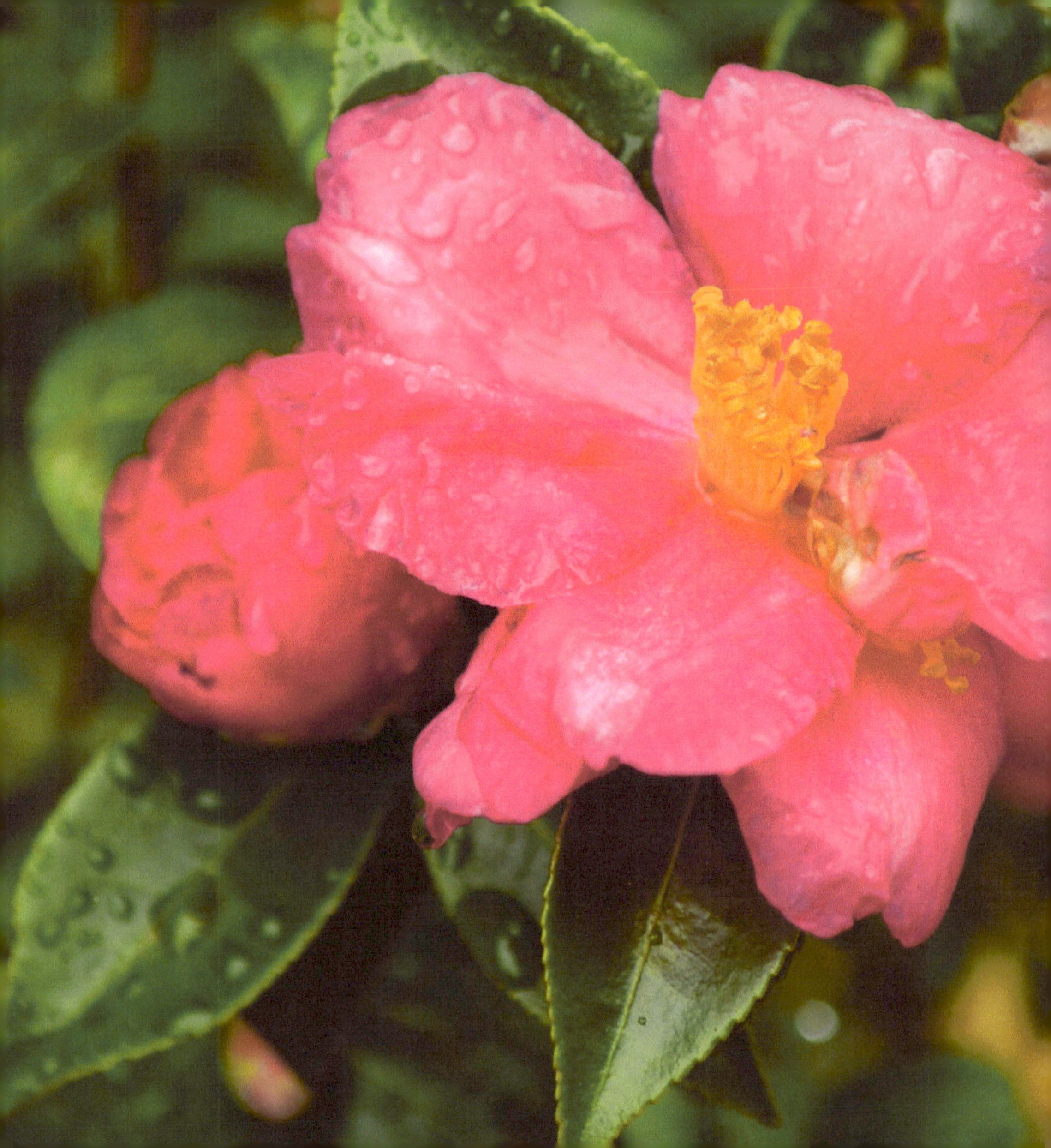

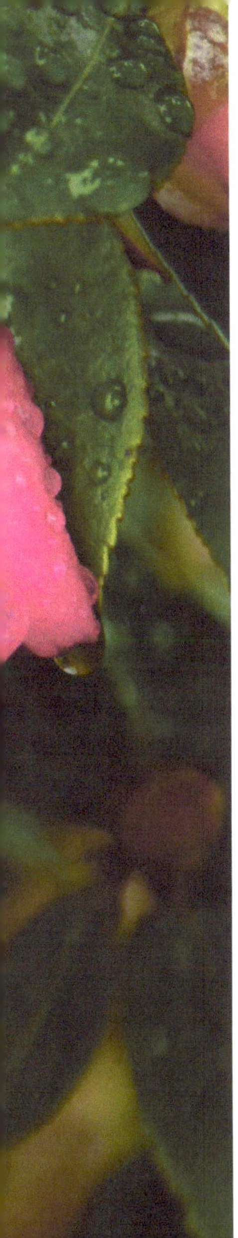

"Flowers only bloom for a season, but the flowers of your life should be blooming every day. Allow others to smell the fragrance and the goodness in your life as you embrace life with them and through Him."

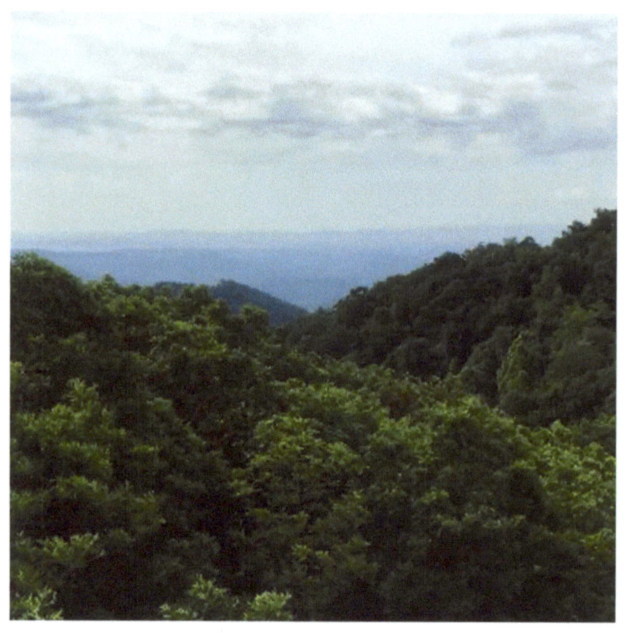

"You can overcome anything. You will overcome. Just stop, listen and pray!"

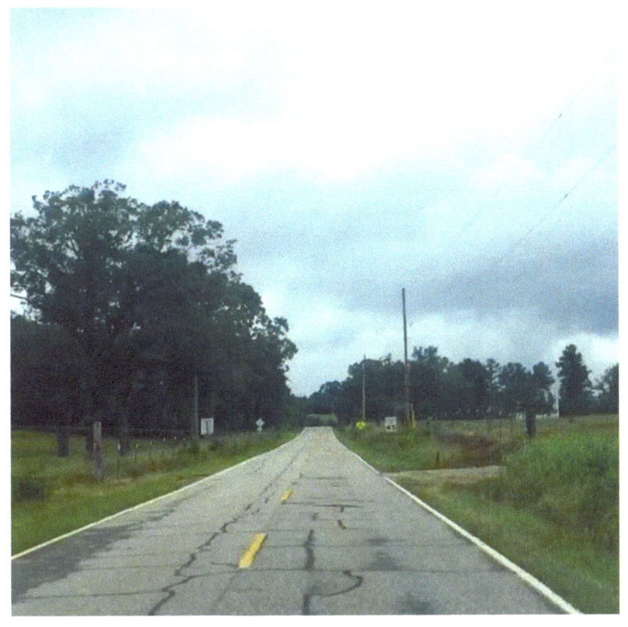

"The road can be lonely as we look around for help. Remember to keep driving to reach your dreams. You may have to do it alone, but keep going and you will arrive."

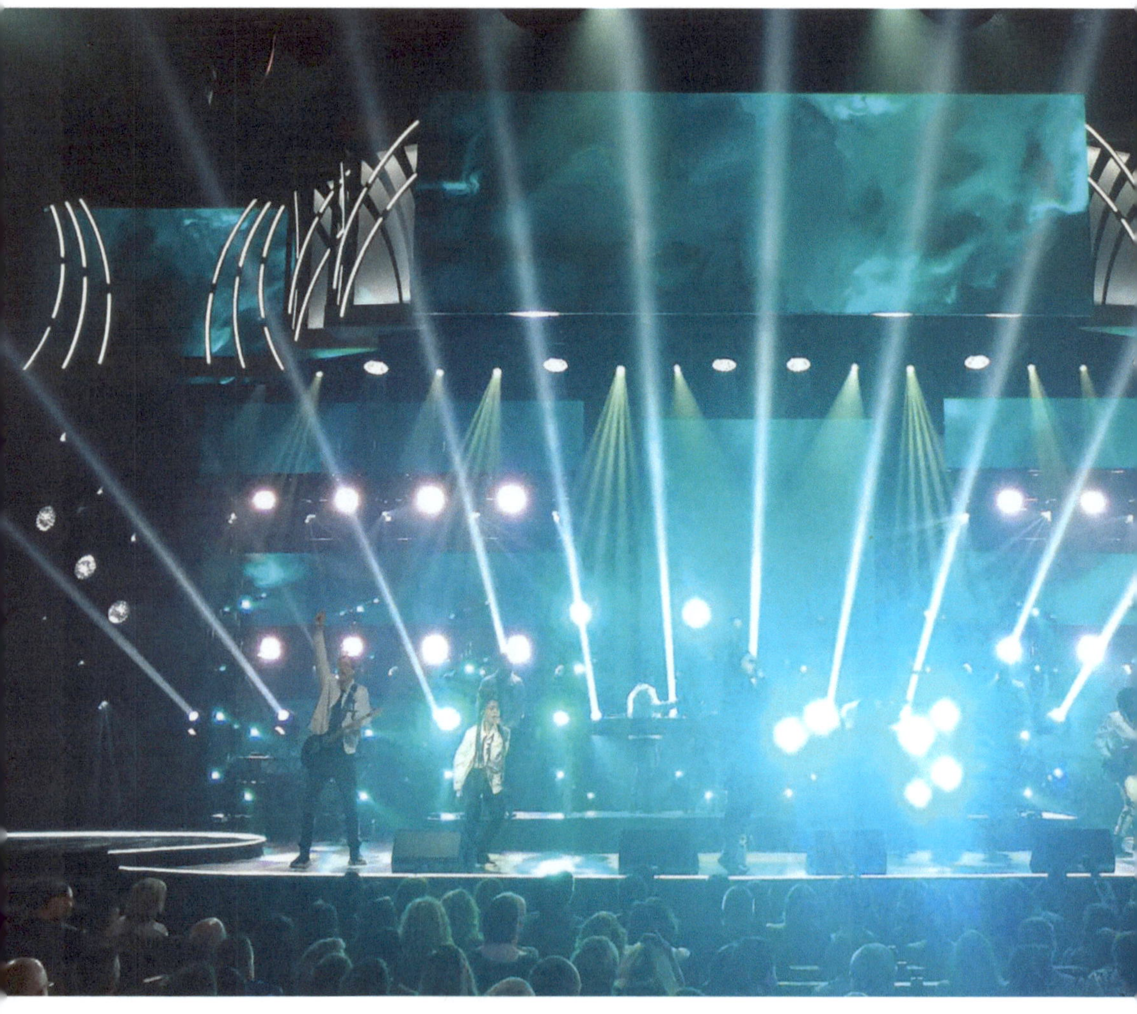

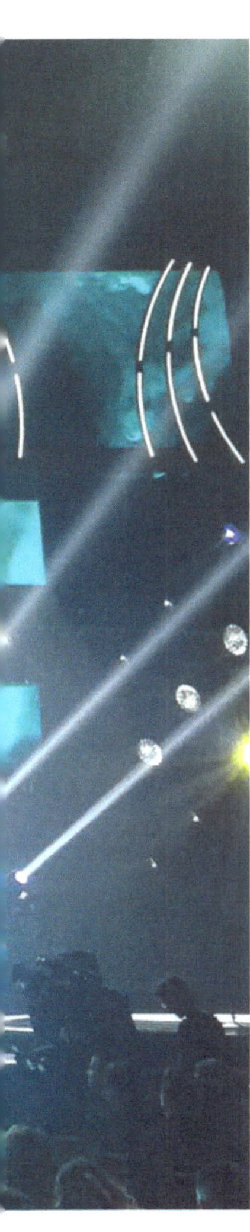

"Follow your HEART and DREAMS. There will always be enough LIGHT to show you the way."

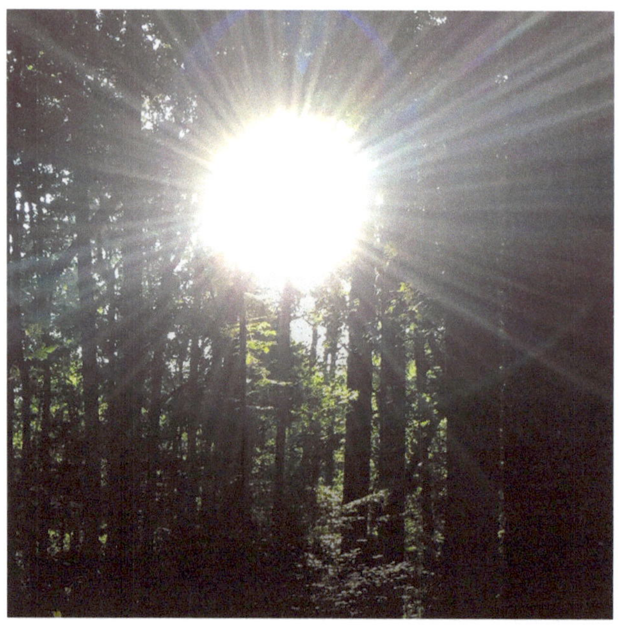

"The sun is always there. It may be hiding for a moment in life, but just wait. Your day will come and it will shine on you, brighter than ever before. Be confident in this."

"Sometimes, things seem so far away and the journey may be long. Keep the faith. You will see the mountain top in the distance and you will arrive soon if you stay on the right path."

"No matter the circumstances, God always shows up in a magnificent way."

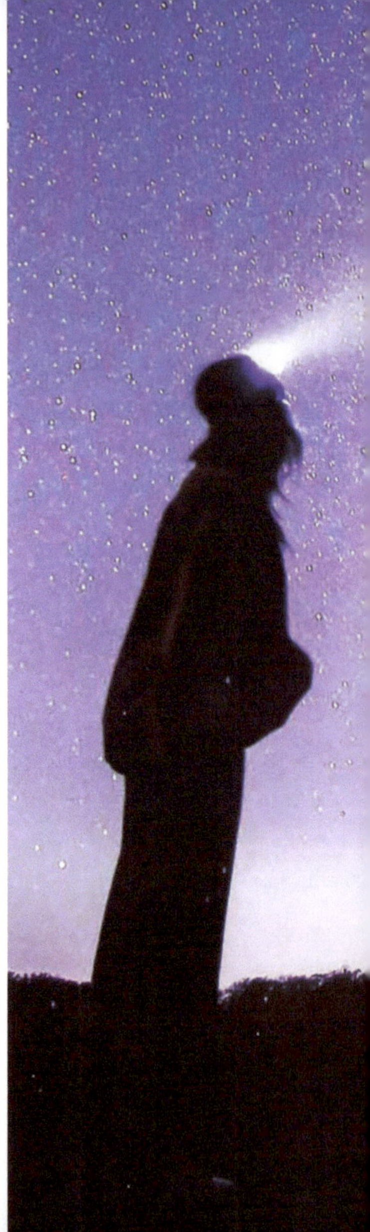

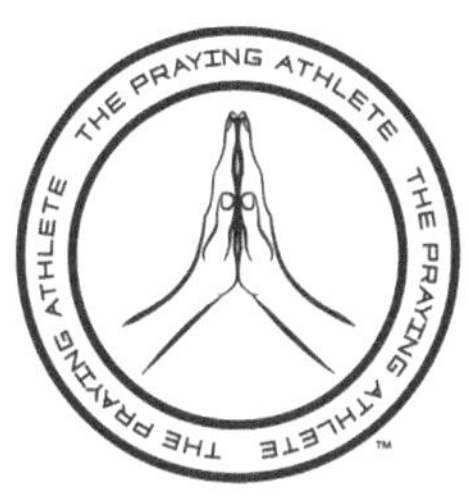

ABOUT TPA

The Praying Athlete is a movement that creates an organic culture of prayer through an uplifting community and authentic conversation.

For more information, visit our website **www.theprayingathlete.com**.

Follow us on social media.

 **@ThePrayingAthlete**

 **@Praying_Athlete**

 **@ThePrayingAthlete**

CHECK OUT OUR
THE PRAYING ATHLETE™
QUOTE BOOK SERIES

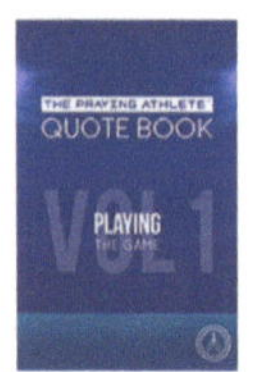

Our first volume of *The Praying Athlete Quote Book* addresses the topic of playing the game. Quotes and thoughts from Robert B. Walker, paired with Scripture from God's Word, allow readers to get a good idea about what playing a good game looks like.

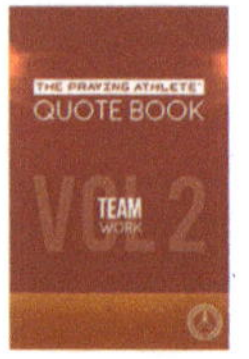

Our second volume of *The Praying Athlete Quote Book* addresses the topic of teamwork. Quotes and thoughts from Robert B. Walker, paired with Scripture from God's Word, allow readers to understand what it means to be a good teammate and surround yourself with people who lift you up.

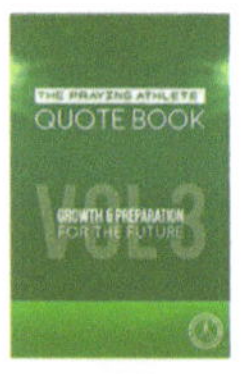

Our third volume of *The Praying Athlete Quote Book* addresses the topic of growth & preparation for the future. Quotes and thoughts from Robert B. Walker, paired with Scripture from God's Word, allow readers to know that even though the future is uncertain, there is a plan and purpose for everyone.

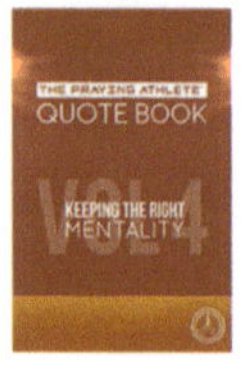

Our fourth volume of *The Praying Athlete Quote Book* addresses the topic of keeping the right mentality. Quotes and thoughts from Robert B. Walker allow readers to understand how staying in the right mindset can improve overall performance.

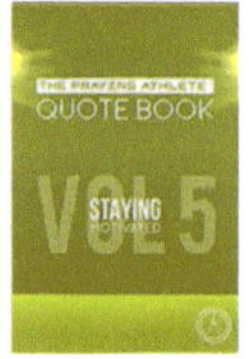

Our fifth volume of *The Praying Athlete Quote Book* addresses the topic of staying motivated. Quotes and thoughts from Robert B. Walker allow readers to become motivated to accomplish their goals, even when they feel they are not up to the task.

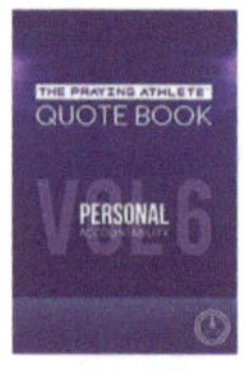

Our sixth volume of *The Praying Athlete Quote Book* addresses the topic of personal accountability. Quotes and thoughts from Robert B. Walker allow readers to think about how they can better themselves. Whether its ending a bad habit or saying no to anything that may hurt themselves or others, staying accountable will benefit one's character and performance.

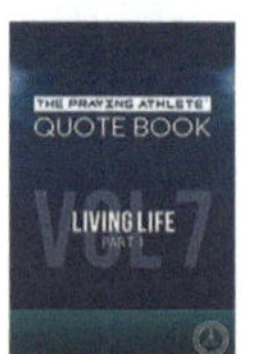

Our seventh volume of *The Praying Athlete Quote Book* addresses the topic of living life. This volume is the first part in a two part living life series. Quotes and thoughts from Robert B. Walker give readers a better understanding of how to live life to the fullest.

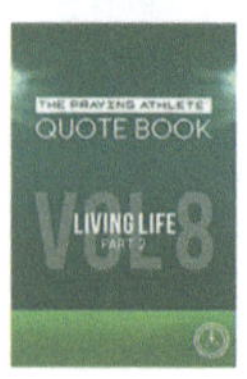

Our eighth volume of *The Praying Athlete Quote Book* addresses the topic of living life. This volume is the second part in a two part living life series. Quotes and thoughts from Robert B. Walker give readers a better understanding of how to live life to the fullest.

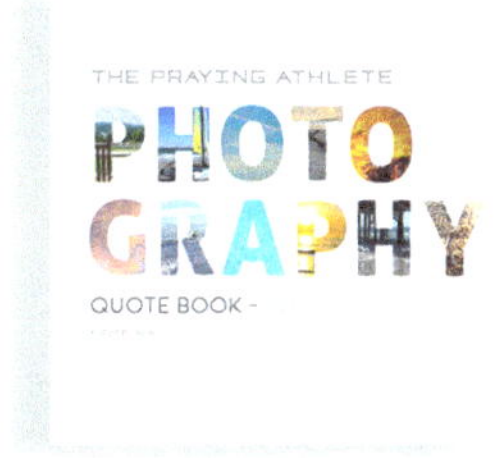

VOL. 1

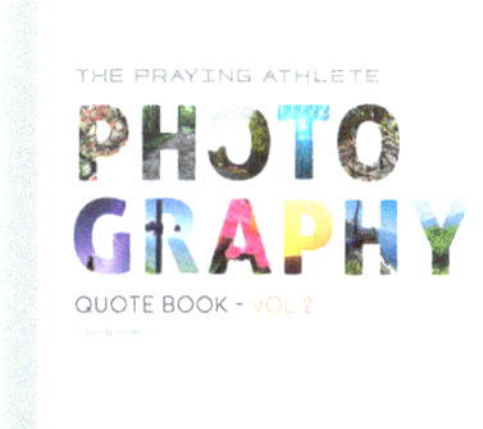

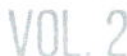
VOL. 2

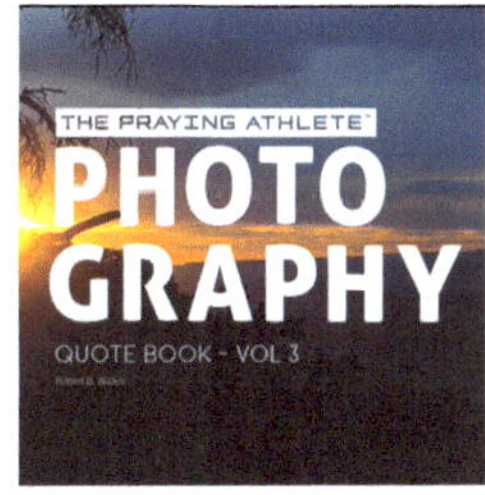

VOL. 3

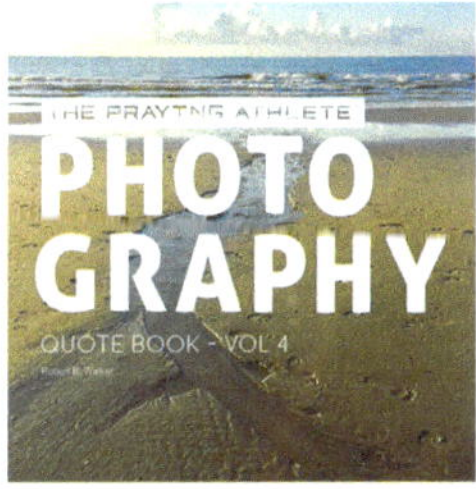

VOL. 4

The Praying Athlete Photography Quote Books celebrate God's glory and magnificence through His creation. They contain photos taken by Robert B. Walker, paired with his words of wisdom, motivation, and inspiration.

www.ingramcontent.com/pod-product-compliance
Lightning Source LLC
LaVergne TN
LVHW070156110826
845147LV00002B/420

* 9 7 8 1 9 5 0 4 6 5 1 4 9 *